G000066214

THIRTY
SPANISH POEMS
OF
LOVE AND EXILE

KENNETH REXROTH

THE POCKET POETS SERIES
Number Two
CITY LIGHTS BOOKS
San Francisco

Library of Congress Catalog Card Number: 55-12235

Sixth Printing

The Pocket Poets Series is published at the City Lights Book Shop, 261 Columbus Avenue, San Francisco 11, and distributed in Great Britain and Europe by The Scorpion Press, 11 Rofant Road, Northwood, Middlesex, England.

INTRODUCTION

Only some of these poets were born in Spain. None of them lives there today.

RAFAEL ALBERTI (1902-) is considered by many to be Spain's leading living poet, very close to being the equal of Garcia Lorca. These *Ritornos* or Homecomings are from his most recent book — a cry of pain in exile.

MARIANO BRULL (1891-) is a Cuban. For many years he has been a diplomat, with posts all over the world. He somewhat resembles our Wallace Stevens.

NICOLAS GUILLEN (1902-) is the leading ' Afro-Cuban ' poet. Since the War he has been travelling widely, especially in the Balkans, Russia, and China, where he is very popular.

PABLO NERUDA (1904-) is a Chilean. He is almost certainly the leading poet of his type alive, a finer writer than Aragon, and the equal of Mayakofsky, if not of Eluard. He has recently reissued the love poems written in his youth, and they have been creating quite a sensation.

ARTURO SERRANO PLAJA (1909-) now lives in exile in France after years of wandering.

The *cancioneros* are given to show their influence on all modern Spanish poetry — especially Lorca and Machado, but even Guillen. The two Lorca poems are essentially modern *cancioneros,* which is why I have given them. Garcia Lorca of course needs no introduction.

ANTONIO MACHADO (1875-1939) is, in my opinion, the finest of the poets of the generation of the '90s. His influence has been tremendous.

KENNETH REXROTH

CONTENTS

HOMECOMING OF LOVE
ON THE SUMMITS OF THE WIND

Here you are, my love, preceded by the wind
Which gushes over the blonde plains where bread suddenly
Blossomed in the warm hours
Of our first summer,
Climbing high into the light amongst the stones.

You rock in the narrow cradle of the ruins
Of parallel arches which Roman hands
Stretched around these temples and towers
Of their town, hoping someday maybe
You would crown them with your delicate steps
Of burning whiteness.

You take to yourself, in the midst of the murmuring stones,
And the sonorous bones locked away in their hollows,
The face of light rising up over the bald mountains,
The villages of faded bricks.
The burning paths, the vast drowsiness
Of a landscape astonished at the sight of you —
Rising like an apparition on the summit of the wind.

O my love, if I could only see you once more
Unawares, as in the old days,
Under that high sun which gave the hours
Of our first summer their harmony.
All that bright, luminous music which you were,
Rocking there in the cradle of ancient stones.

                                        RAFAEL ALBERTI

HOMECOMING OF LOVE
ON A RAINY EVENING

Once more it is raining and cloudy
On the days of my dead and
My still living, deathless years.
Rain falls once more on the pinewoods through the fog.
Rain, gale, thunderclaps
Like far off distant cheering,
And the final whipcracks of lightning on the peaks.
The same white old woman reveals herself once more,
Rising from her bed clothes,
Warmed by babies and their sweet eyes.
And my mother appears in the stained glass
Of the high oriel which reveals
Once more that blue city of snowy shadows
And green balustrades, where,
Suddenly once more in the evening,
Fingers which the sea abandoned
Secretly and forgetfully to the breeze
Echo once more in the evening.
And so once more I will go out
For a walk with Agustin and Jose Ignacio
And Paquito, the sons of the coachman.
And we will hunt for snails on the walls,
Amongst the yellow flowers, among the tombs,
Or else we will go once more
Across the lost forest of broom thickets,
And play bullfighter with the new calves
And the youngsters will show me up.

Ghost squalls which come unawares from nowhere,
Rapid conversations of the forests,
The broken dialogue, the confidences
Of the sea and the soaking sands.
I bow my head.
I cup my ear in my hand.
I try to understand the message of the waves
Of the mingling distant roar and the nearby wash.
I hear far off hoof beats
Wearing away the castle walls
Of the drowned ruins, the stairways
That go down into the sea surge.
I know who goes there. I know the unbridled rider,
Singing on his runaway black colt of salt and foam
Where is he running? Where is he running?
Towards what submarine gates? Through what portals
Of moving azure? Into what bright interiors?
He seeks a profile, a material form,
A line, a color, a figure, a music,
Tangible, definite.
He seeks for the archways, the lintels
Which lead to unclouded villages,
Harmonious frontiers, precise firmaments,
Cloudless skies,
Paradises without smoke.
Under the rain the sea has vanished,
Disappeared, the sea is gone,
Has been obliterated by the fog. Soon
It will have carried away the woods, too, and these tree trunks
They will go easily,
Without a quiver in all their height to tell me
That they are dead. That my eyes

Are dead, this evening full of fog and rain.
Who does see in this darkness?
Who is it who tries to merge with the shadows?
Who tries to make this starless night grow solid?
The sea is dead. The sea is dead. And with it, once more
All byegone things. It waits.
It alone waits, all alone, do you understand?
A confused conversation, a wandering
Gossip, without audible words, an
Invading horror,
For one who returns eyeless, eyes closed without sleep.

RAFAEL ALBERTI

HOMECOMING OF LOVE
IN THE MIDST OF THE SEA

My splendor, my love,
Beginning of my life,
I want to tell all of your beauty,
Here, in the midst of the sea, while I seek for you,
While I have only the cool beauty
Of the waves to compare with you.
Your hair is a fountain of gold,
A rain of foam embracing me,
Bearing me up, to sail to the end of the night.
Your brow is the dawn above double rainbows,
Where the suns go by so gently
Like boats dreaming into the daybreak.

What can I say about your mouth, your ears,
Your neck, your shoulders; when the sea hides its shells,
Its coral and submarine gardens,
Lest, under the wings of the South,
I compare them to you?
Your thighs are like two long still bays.
The silence of love envelops them.
They sing the same song as your arms.
It is sad to have to say this, here, far away
From those shadowy gulfs, those islands
Calling to a sail they sense passing by,
Far from its route, unseen.
My love, your legs are two beaches,
Two taut, undulant dunes,
Rumorous with rushes when they are not sleeping.
Give me your little feet to caress,
Let me know all your shores,
Let me sink into the sea, let me sink into you, my life,
Into your love, through your love, singing
Of your beauty, beautiful as the waves.

RAFAEL ALBERTI

HOMECOMING OF LOVE
IN A NIGHT OF SORROW

Come, my love, come, in this lonely,
Sad Italian night. Here are your shoulders,
Strong and lovely as I need them to be.
Here are your precious arms, the proud
Swell of your buttocks, the spring

Of your legs, the compact line which
Turns about you and suspends you —
My happy sea, my open shore.
What is there to say, my love, in this lonely
Night in Genoa, listening
To the blue heart of the surf beating?
It is you I hear coming to me through the foam.
Kiss me, my love, here in the unhappy night.
I will tell you, my love, those words
Which my lips, full of love, never dared say.
My love, my love, here is your golden head,
Leaning against me, here is your burning
Autumnal forest listening to me.
Hear me, I call you, my life,
Yes, my life, my only life.
Who else? Who else? Only I
Am able to sing for your ears.
O life, my life, my own life!
What do I amount to without you? My love, tell me.
What would become of me without this powerful and tender
Wall which gives me my light when it casts your shadow on me,
And sleep when it withdraws from my eyes?
I cannot sleep. How many dark dawns
Will wave their arms in the shadows
Before I see you once more, my love? And all the gulps
Of bitter salt against my mouth.
Where are you? Where are you? Tell me, my love!
Can you hear me? Can't you feel me,
Coming to you like a tear, calling you,
Beyond the sea, in the night?

RAFAEL ALBERTI

HOMECOMING OF LOVE
IN A SUMMER NIGHT

Love comes, blindly groping its way in the dark,
Like a star ripening amongst the branches.
It comes, I can feel it come,
Drenched with the chilling frost of night
Through the gap cut in the thyme and mint.

It is he, the only, the unique, the one of my hand,
Of the skin that stretches over my flesh, the shadow
Of my new born heart, of my dark crossroads,
Of my far off, underground intersections.

He comes back, the unique, he comes back.
O scarcely touched form, an overflowing
Palpitation, tight, covered with hair,
O blood mixed with my blood. the heartbeat
Heard in the interior of another heartbeat.

But words — where are the words?
The words do not come. They are lost in space
In the exhausted night. They are lost
In this least bit of air separating two mouths
Before it shrinks to a flower of silence.

An occult perfume spreads, glides through the air,
The odor of a dark shore awakens me, burns me,
Someone comes, lighting a murmur in the grasses.
Someone crosses a river in the night of love.

                              RAFAEL ALBERTI

HOMECOMING OF LOVE
ON THE SANDS

This morning. my love, we are twenty years old.
Let us go, very slowly, braiding together
Our barefoot shadows, on paths through orchards
That face the blue of the sea with all their greenness.
You are almost an apparition,
The same one which came once in the lightless evening
Between two lights,
When the young citizen, pensive and idle,
Loitered along his homeward road.
You are still the one seeking, beside me,
The steep secret of the dunes,
The hidden slope of sand, the occult
Reeds which hold
Their curtains before the sea eyes of the wind.
You are there. I am there beside you. I control
The vast temperature of the happy waves,
The heart of the sea, blindly rising,
And dying in tatters of foam and sweet salt.
The collapsing castles rear their battlements,
The seaweeds offer us their crowns, the sails
Tense in flight, sing over the towers.

This morning, my love, we are twenty years old.
                                      RAFAEL ALBERTI

HOMECOMING OF LOVE
AMONGST ILLUSTRIOUS RUINS

The calcined stones come back.
The fallen temples come back,
The bursted whore houses, the green courtyards
Where the smile of Priapus
Keeps warm the memory of fountains.

My love, let us go along the vanished streets,
Across the bright geometry which still points
To mysterious love and hidden
Pleasures, still so sweet in the night.

Here is the house of the goddess. In the blue
Sanctuary you can still smell the perfume
Of sea foam and jasmine and
Carnations salty with her flesh.

The phallic symbol, jolly as ever,
Riots in the thick foliage — stretched out
On the happy pan of the balance
Which offers it to love. It is heavier
Than all the fruits of the earth.
Aphrodite smiles in the shadows
As she feels the sea throb in her buttocks.

O ancient brightness! O far off light!
Naked light, love, shine on us always.
And when the day comes when we are no more than stones,
After we too, my love, are only ruins,
Let us lie like these stones singing in the sun,
Leading others to love along our vanished ways.

RAFAEL ALBERTI

THE NAMING DAWN

Smooth, rosy, importunate,
The daybreak was giving you names:
Equivocal Dream, Aimless Angel,
Lying Rain on the Forest.

On the boundaries of my soul
Which remembers the rivers,
Indecisive, doubting, immobile:
Spilled Star, Light Confused in Tears,
Voiceless Crystal?

No.
Error of Snow on Water, your name.

RAFAEL ALBERTI

NAKED

Her whole body resounds in the mirror,
Articulate in distant images,
One and multiple, thick, reflected,
Reversed, the now in the immediate past.

Back from its anterior flight
It returns trembling to the semblance of itself.
Retained, dispersed, to the distance
Of two voices, two looks, two instants.

Its total absence is there in its presence,
Prolonged until the next approach
Of the imminent start of another absence.

Intact road in the pathless void,
For the immobile hazard of her will,
— Statue of her body to come.

MARIANO BRULL

SOLO OF NIGHT

This night comes out of that night
Like an exact mold
Of the first night —
And the sky and the stars and the moon
Are finished and born for this night.
This sky is an exact copy of that sky,

This star of that star, this moon
The tracing of that new moon —
This night, graven on the picture of that night.
It lights its lights.
It puts out its lights.
The horizon undulates its vast back
Into the architectural air of heaven.
The town that voyaged in the air
Returns to its wandering soil.
And the urban skyline lifts up the same towers.
Each shadow has its place, each star its light.
The flower returns to the flower, the hour to the hour.

And the night, alone with the night.

MARIANO BRULL

A ROSE IN A VASE

This library has its own solitude.
A corner casts a cone of shadow.
Whirling, turning,
The dust motes glimmer.
The table with a quiet explosion
Interrupts the soft penumbra
With the brusque clarity of a circle.
In its vase, the rose, smooth and cool,
Guards its own dream.
The topmost petal on its crest of light
Draws on the sky the eye of a rose.

Breaking the veins of transparence,
Water and crystal
Contemplate their diaphanous secrets.

MARIANO BRULL

YOU, MELANCHOLY ROSE

My soul flies and flies,
Seeking you far away,
Melancholy Rose,
Rose of memory.
When early morning
Dampens the meadow
And dawn is a child
Waking up in the sky,
Melancholy Rose,
Eyes filled with darkness.
In my narrow bed
I stroke your firm body.
And while the high sun
Burns with its high fire,
And while evening falls
Into broken twilight,
Here at my far off table
I contemplate your dark bread.
And in the night
Full of devouring silence,
Melancholy Rose,
Rose of memory,

14

Golden, alive, moist,
You come down over the roof tops
And take my freezing hand
And hold me fast.
I shut my eyes
So I can keep your face
Nailed down here, nailing
Your gaze into my breast,
Your long still glance
Like a stab in a dream.

NICOLAS GUILLEN

A LITTLE BALLAD
OF PLOVDIV

In the old town of Plovdiv,
Far away,
My heart went out one night,
That's all.

A long green glance,
Far away,
Wet lips saying no.
That's all.

The shining bulgar sky,
Far away,
Full of trembling stars,
That's all.

Oh, slow steps in the street,
Far away,
The last steps forever,
That's all.

By the mysterious harbor,
Far away,
A white hand, one kiss,
That's all.

NICOLAS GUILLEN

MADRIGAL

Your womb is smarter than your head,
And as smart as your bottom.
See —
The fierce black grace
Of your naked body.

You are the symbol of the forest,
With your red necklaces,
Your bracelets of curving gold,
And the dark alligator
Swimming in the Zambezi of your eyes.

NICOLAS GUILLEN

SATCHELMOUTH

What you mad about?
Cause they call you Satchelmouth?
You know you got sweet lips,
Satchelmouth.

Satchelmouth, that's you.
You've got it.
Your old lady keeps you nice.
Cause you give her all of it.

What you moaning about?
Satchelmouth.
Lots of gold and no work.
Satchelmouth.
Fancy white shirts.
Satchelmouth.
Two tone shoes,
Satchelmouth.

Satchelmouth,
That's you. You've got it.
And your old lady keeps you
Cause you give it all to her.

NICOLAS GUILLEN

BROWN AND AGILE CHILD

Brown and agile child, the sun which forms the fruit
And ripens the grain and twists the seaweed
Has made your happy body and your luminous eyes
And given your mouth the smile of water.

A black and anguished sun is entangled in the twigs
Of your black mane when you hold out your arms.
You play in the sun as in a tidal river
And it leaves two dark pools in your eyes.

Brown and agile child, nothing draws me to you,
Everything pulls away from me here in the noon.
You are the delirious youth of the bee,
The drunkenness of the wave, the power in the wheat.

My somber heart seeks you always,
I love your happy body, your rich, soft voice,
Dusky butterfly, sweet and sure
Like the wheatfield, the sun, the poppy, and the water.

                    PABLO NERUDA

SERENADE

I believe you are more mine than my skin. When I seek
Within me, along my veins, in my blood, my mysterious
Circulatory branches of light that I tell over,
It is you I find, as if you were blood,
As if you were stone or a bite.
I stay outside late, reason, delirium, clothes.
I am of an old race of darkness and forests,
But while I bend down as in a well and enter
Feeling my way like a blind man in my own territory,
I find no railing to direct my steps,
But, instead, the growth of your rose in my own dwelling.

Deep in me you go on growing, unfathomable
In your origin, I cannot touch your eyes
Without burning my fingernails on their petals,
The flames of your form which burn in my thirst,
The leaves of your face which build your absence.
I ask, ' Who is there? Who is there?' as if very late,
Very late, somebody knocked
On my door, and then in the middle
Of emptiness there was nothing but air,
Water, trees, the dying daily fire,
As if there was nothing there but everything which exists,
Nothing but all the earth which had rapped on my door.
So, nameless, vague as life, turbid
As the burgeoning mud and vegetation,
You awake in my breast whenever I shut my eyes.
When I lie on the earth you come into being
Like the flowing dust, the river deepening its bed,
Guarding a tangle of naked roots
Which grows as grows your presence in me,
Which accompanies their darkness as you accompany me.
So, here, blood or wheat, earth or fire, we live
Like a single plant which cannot explain its leaves.

PABLO NERUDA

POEM

I remember you as you were that last autumn —
Your grey beret, your calm heart,
And the flames of sunset wrestling in your eyes,
And the leaves falling into the waters of your soul.

You clung to my arm like a vine.
The leaves caught up your slow calm voice —
Vertiginous hearth where my heart blazes —
Sweet blue hyacinth twisting over my soul.

I can feel your eyes, voyaging away, distant as that autumn,
Grey beret, voice of a bird, heart of a huntress —
Where all my deep agony migrated,
Where my happy kisses fell like embers.

The skies from shipboard. Fields from the hills.
Your memory is of light, of smoke, of a still pool.
Deep in your eyes the twilights burned.
The dry leaves of autumn whirled in your soul.

PABLO NERUDA

POEM

The light envelops you in its mortal flame.
Faint, pale, sad, you stand
Against the old spirals of twilight
As they revolve around you.

My love, mute,
Alone in the solitude of this hour of dying,
Full of the lives of the fire,
Pure heiress of the shattered day.

A cluster falls from the sun onto your dark dress.
The vast roots of night
Burst forth from your soul.
And all that was hidden in you rises to the surface.
It is a pale blue city
That you have borne and nourished.

Oh grandiose, fecund and magnetic slave
Of the circle where black and gold revolve —
She pitches her tent and produces a creation so alive
That her flowers die and her sorrow overflows.

PABLO NERUDA

SPRING

Here by the bridges of the Seine
In this spring of exile
I know I am old at last and alone with my pain.
And I feel the weight of the chain
Of all my dilapidated liberty.

Here I am, a knotted and wormeaten trunk,
Stripped leafless in this winter country.
And now there come to my branches
And to my trunk of forgetfulness,
So lightly, the morning sparrows
And begin to build a nest.

Here I am, bridge to another age —
And in the current, bye gone, raw memories,
Like melting snow
Under a burning sun,
Pass away beneath my eyes
And leave only their reflections
Like brilliant light in a mirror.

ARTURO SERRANO PLAJA

AUTUMN

Is this autumn with its color of forgetfulness,
Its yellow gestures in the tender twilight?
Can this be the same valley which waited for winter,
Gathering its quiet about it, its sadness?

Is this calm pine offering to teach me?
These silver poplars along the river bank?
Or the far off golden woodland telling over and over
With the ink of dead leaves the mystery of the temple?

Maybe this heavy, trembling weakness
Of passing fever, of a convalescence,
Which ties me to life with strands of patience,
Offers me, in place of bitter hope, this enchantment?

Today everything is yellow, trembling and distant,
And the seas still wait for me, although I am still uprooted,
Although the wanderings of exile,
With their abandoned dreams, still lie ahead of me,
Today there is only the splendor of peace and melody.

ARTURO SERRANO PLAJA

LETRILLA-CANCIONERO

When the wind murmurs
Mother, in the leaves,
The drone puts me to sleep
Deep in the shade.

The calm wind blows
Lightly, softly,
And moves the ship
Of my mind.
I am so contented.
It seems to me
Heaven has given me
Too many blessings.
And the drone puts me to sleep
Deep in the shade.

If I happen to wake up
Covered with flowers
I cannot remember
Anything sorrowful.
All trace of my loss
Is hidden in dreams.
And new life comes
In the sound of the leaves.
And the drone puts me to sleep
Deep in the shade.

                              — **Early Anonymous**

CANCIONERO

Come at dawn, beloved.
Come at dawn.

Lover, I want you the most.
Come at the dawn of day.

Lover, I love you the most.
Come at the break of day.

Come at the break of day.
Don't bring anybody.

Come at the light of dawn.
Come, all alone.

— Early Anonymous

CANCIONERO

I loved three Moorish girls
In Jaen —
Axa, Fatima, Marien.

Three graceful Moorish girls,
Who went to pick olives,
And found them all picked,
In Jaen —
Axa, Fatima, Marien.

24

Three lively Moorish girls,
Three lively Moorish girls
Went to pick apples
In Jaen —
Axa, Fatima, Marien.

— Early Anonymous

L O L A

Under the orange tree,
She washes her underwear.
Her eyes are very green.
Her voice is violet.

Ha! Love,
Under the orange blossoms!

The water in the brook
Is full of the sun.
In the olive tree
A sparrow is singing.

Ha! Love,
Under the orange blossoms!

As soon as Lola
Uses up her soap,
Some guys show up.

Ha! Love,
Under the orange blossoms!

FEDERICO GARCIA LORCA

THE WEEPING

I have shut my windows.
I do not want to hear the weeping.
But from behind the grey walls,
Nothing is heard but the weeping.

There are few angels that sing.
There are few dogs that bark.
A thousand violins fit in the palm of the hand.
But the weeping is an immense angel.
The weeping is an immense dog.
The weeping is an immense violin.
Tears strangle the wind.
Nothing is heard but the weeping.

FEDERICO GARCIA LORCA

POEM

Green little gardens,
Bright little squares,
Verdigris fountains,
Where water dreams,
Where mute water
Slips over stone.

Leaves of faded
Green, almost black,
Of the acacias — the wind

Of September has
Stripped their flowers
And carried a few,
Yellow and dry,
To play there in the white
Dust of the earth.

Pretty girl,
Filling your pitcher
With transparent water,
When you catch sight of me you don't
Lift your brown hand
And arrange the black curls
Ot your hair
And admire yourself
In the limpid crystal.

You gaze into the air
Of the beautiful evening
While the clear water
Fills your pitcher.

ANTONIO MACHADO

POEM

It is not true, sorrow, that I have known you.
You are the nostaglia of a good life,
The solitude of a somber heart,
A boat without shipwreck and without star.

Like a lost dog, wandering,
Sniffing and hunting aimlessly
For his road, without a road, like
A child on a holiday night

Lost among the crowds,
The dusty air, the flickering
Candles, stunned, his heart drunk
With music and hurt,

So I go, drunk and melancholy,
Lunatic guitarist, poet,
A poor man in a dream,
Hunting for God in the mists.

ANTONIO MACHADO

NOTES

I

Out of my window —
The fields of Baeza
Under the full moon,
The mountains of Cazorla,
Aznaitin and Magina,

Moonlight and stone,
And the lion cubs
Of the Sierra Morena.

II
In the olive grove
I can see an owl
Flying and flying.

Fields. Fields. Fields.
Amongst the olives,
The white farm houses.

And the black oak
In the middle of the road
Between Ubeda and Baeza.

III
Through the stained glass
The owl got into
The cathedral.

Saint Christopher
Wanted to chase her away
Because she tried to drink
The oil from the lamp
Of Saint Mary.

But the Virgin said —
' Let her drink,
Saint Christopher.'

IV
In the olive grove
I can see the owl
Flying and flying.

She flies heavily
Carrying a green branch
To Saint Mary.

Fields of Baeza
I will dream of you
When I can see you no more.

ANTONIO MACHADO

SONGS

I
Against the flowering mountain
The full seas dash.
The wax of my bees
Holds little grains of salt.

II
Spring has come.
Nobody knows how it did it.

III
Full moon, full moon,
So full, so round,

On this serene night
Of March; wax of light
Made by white bees.

ANTONIO MACHADO

POEM

O solitude, my only companion,
O muse of portents, who has given
My voice words I could never ask for,
Answer my question — Who do I speak to?

Absent from the noisy masquerade,
Diverting my sorrow without a friend,
Always close to you, lady with veiled face,
Always veiled during our dialogues.

Today I think — What does it matter who I am?
This is not the gravest enigma — this face
Which recreates itself in my intimate mirror,

But the mystery of your loving voice.
Uncover your features so I can see,
Fixed on me, your diamond eyes.

ANTONIO MACHADO

MEDITATION FOR THIS DAY

Facing the palm of fire
Which spreads from the departing sun
Throughout the silent evening —
In this garden of peace —
While flowery Valencia
Drinks the Guadalquiver —
Valencia of slender towers
In the young skies of Ausias March,
Your river changes to roses
At the touch of the sea.
I think of the war. War
Has swept like a tornado
Through the steppes of high Douro,
Through the plains of growing bread,
From fertile Estramadura
To the gardens of lemon trees,
From the grey skies of Asturias
To the marshes of light and salt.
I think that Spain has been sold out,
River by river, mountain by mountain, sea by sea.

ANTONIO MACHADO